20 best
cookie contest
recipes

Houghton Mifflin Harcourt
Boston • New York • 2013

Copyright © 2013 by General Mills, Minneapolis, Minnesota. All rights reserved.

For information about permission to reproduce selections from this book, write to Permissions, Houghton Mifflin Harcourt Publishing Company, 215 Park Avenue South, New York, New York 10003.

www.hmhco.com

Cover photo: Red Velvet Rich-and-Creamy Cookies (page 9)

General Mills
Food Content and Relationship Marketing Director: Geoff Johnson
Food Content Marketing Manager: Susan Klobuchar
Senior Editor: Grace Wells
Kitchen Manager: Ann Stuart
Recipe Development and Testing: Betty Crocker Kitchens
Photography: General Mills Photography Studios and Image Library

Houghton Mifflin Harcourt
Publisher: Natalie Chapman
Editorial Director: Cindy Kitchel
Executive Editor: Anne Ficklen
Associate Editor: Heather Dabah
Managing Editor: Rebecca Springer
Production Editor: Kristi Hart
Cover Design: Chrissy Kurpeski
Book Design: Tai Blanche

ISBN 978-0-544-31474-0
Printed in the United States of America

The Betty Crocker Kitchens seal guarantees success in your kitchen. Every recipe has been tested in America's Most Trusted Kitchens™ to meet our high standards of reliability, easy preparation and great taste.

FIND MORE GREAT IDEAS AT
Betty Crocker.com

Dear Friends,

This new collection of colorful mini books has been put together with you in mind because we know that you love great recipes and enjoy cooking and baking but have a busy lifestyle. So every little book in the series contains just 20 recipes for you to treasure and enjoy. Plus, each book is a single subject designed in a bite-size format just for you—it's easy to use and is filled with favorite recipes from the Betty Crocker Kitchens!

All of the books are conveniently divided into short chapters so you can quickly find what you're looking for, and the beautiful photos throughout are sure to entice you into making the delicious recipes. In the series, you'll discover a fabulous array of recipes to spark your interest—from cookies, cupcakes and birthday cakes to party ideas for a variety of occasions. There's grilled foods, potluck favorites and even gluten-free recipes too.

You'll love the variety in these mini books—so pick one or choose them all for your cooking pleasure.

Enjoy and happy cooking!

Sincerely,

Betty Crocker

contents

Gooey and Chewy
Mint–Chocolate Chip Cookies • 6
White Chocolate–Cranberry Cookies • 7
Chewy Granola Drops • 8
Red Velvet Rich-and-Creamy Cookies • 9
Ultimate Chocolate-Cappuccino Cookie
    Cups • 10
Best-Ever Chewy Gingerbread Cookies • 11

Chunky and Nutty
Spumoni Chunk Cookies • 12
Choco-Cherry Double Delights • 13
Choco-Hazelnut Latte Cookies • 14
Dark Chocolate–Glazed Orange Macaroons • 15
Butter Pecan Thumbprints • 16
Pumpkin-Pecan Spice Cookies • 17

Crispy and Crunchy
Caramel Macchiato Thumbprints • 18
Black-and-White Coconut Macaroons • 19
Linzer Cookie Tarts • 20
Summer Celebration Lemonade Biscotti • 21
Memory Lane Oatmeal–Peanut Butter
    Creme Sandwiches • 22
Alfajores (Dulce de Leche Sandwich
    Creme Cookies) • 23
Iced Cinnamon-Pecan Biscotti • 24
Mega-Bucks Shortbread • 25

Metric Conversion Guide • 26
Recipe Testing and Calculating Nutrition
    Information • 27

Gooey and Chewy

Mint–Chocolate Chip Cookies

Prep Time: 25 Minutes • **Start to Finish:** 40 Minutes • Makes 3 dozen cookies

1 pouch (1 lb 1.5 oz) Betty Crocker® sugar cookie mix
½ cup butter or margarine, softened
¼ to ½ teaspoon mint extract
6 to 8 drops green food color
1 egg
1 cup crème de menthe baking chips
1 cup semisweet chocolate chunks

{ Cookie Contest Winner **Patti Bullock** }

1 Heat oven to 350°F. In large bowl, stir cookie mix, butter, mint extract, food color and egg until soft dough forms. Stir in baking chips and chocolate chunks.

2 Onto ungreased cookie sheet, drop dough by rounded teaspoonfuls about 2 inches apart.

3 Bake 8 to 10 minutes or until set. Cool 3 minutes; remove from cookie sheets to cooling racks. Store cooled cookies tightly covered at room temperature.

1 Cookie: Calories 130; Total Fat 7g (Saturated Fat 3.5g, Trans Fat 0.5g); Cholesterol 15mg; Sodium 60mg; Total Carbohydrate 16g (Dietary Fiber 0g); Protein 1g **Exchanges:** 1 Other Carbohydrate, 1½ Fat **Carbohydrate Choices:** 1

Tip Use a cookie or ice cream scoop to make same-size cookies for even baking.

White Chocolate–Cranberry Cookies

Prep Time: 55 Minutes • **Start to Finish:** 1 Hour 25 Minutes • Makes 3 dozen cookies

¾ cup butter or margarine, softened

¾ cup packed light brown sugar

½ cup granulated sugar

2 teaspoons vanilla

1 teaspoon almond extract, if desired

1 egg

1¾ cups Gold Medal® all-purpose flour

½ teaspoon baking soda

¼ teaspoon salt

1 cup white vanilla baking chips (6 oz)

1 cup sweetened dried cranberries

{ Cookie Contest Winner **Laura Abeloe** }

1 Heat oven to 350°F. In large bowl, beat butter, brown sugar, granulated sugar, vanilla, almond extract and egg with electric mixer on medium speed until well mixed. Stir in flour, baking soda and salt. Stir in baking chips and cranberries.

2 Onto ungreased cookie sheet, drop dough by rounded tablespoonfuls about 2 inches apart.

3 Bake 12 to 15 minutes or until light brown. Cool 2 to 3 minutes; remove from cookie sheets to cooling racks.

1 Cookie: Calories 130; Total Fat 6g (Saturated Fat 3.5g, Trans Fat 0g); Cholesterol 15mg; Sodium 70mg; Total Carbohydrate 18g (Dietary Fiber 0g); Protein 1g **Exchanges:** ½ Starch, ½ Other Carbohydrate, 1 Fat **Carbohydrate Choices:** 1

Tip When using brown sugar in baking, it's important to firmly pack the brown sugar into the measuring cup for best results.

Chewy Granola Drops

Prep Time: 40 Minutes • **Start to Finish:** 40 Minutes • Makes 2 dozen cookies

- 1 pouch (1 lb 1.5 oz) Betty Crocker oatmeal chocolate chip cookie mix
- ½ cup butter or margarine, melted
- 1 egg
- 1 cup coconut
- ¾ cup dried cranberries
- 1 can (6 oz) honey-roasted almonds (1¼ cups), coarsely chopped

{ Cookie Contest Winner **Becky Miller** }

1 Heat oven to 375°F. In large bowl, stir cookie mix, melted butter and egg until soft dough forms. Stir in coconut, cranberries and almonds.

2 Onto ungreased cookie sheets, drop dough by rounded tablespoonfuls about 2 inches apart. Press with fingers to slightly flatten.

3 Bake 11 to 12 minutes or until edges are golden brown. Cool 2 minutes; remove from cookie sheets to cooling racks. Cool completely. Store covered at room temperature.

1 Cookie: Calories 200; Total Fat 11g (Saturated Fat 5g, Trans Fat 0g); Cholesterol 20mg; Sodium 115mg; Total Carbohydrate 23g (Dietary Fiber 2g); Protein 2g **Exchanges:** ½ Starch, 1 Other Carbohydrate, 2 Fat **Carbohydrate Choices:** 1½

Red Velvet Rich-and-Creamy Cookies

Prep Time: 1 Hour • **Start to Finish:** 1 Hour 15 Minutes • Makes 3 dozen cookies

1 pouch (1 lb 1.5 oz) Betty Crocker sugar cookie mix

⅓ cup unsweetened baking cocoa

¼ cup butter or margarine, softened

¼ cup sour cream

1 tablespoon red food color

1 egg

¾ to 1 cup Betty Crocker Rich & Creamy cream cheese frosting

¼ cup chopped nuts

{ Cookie Contest Winner **Joan Opdahl** }

1 Heat oven to 375°F. In large bowl, stir cookie mix, cocoa, butter, sour cream, food color and egg until soft dough forms.

2 Shape dough into 1-inch balls. Onto ungreased cookie sheets, place balls about 2 inches apart.

3 Bake 8 to 9 minutes or until set. Cool 2 minutes; remove from cookie sheets to cooling racks. Cool completely, about 15 minutes.

4 Frost cooled cookies with frosting. Sprinkle with nuts. Store tightly covered at room temperature.

1 Cookie: Calories 110; Total Fat 4.5g (Saturated Fat 1.5g, Trans Fat 1g); Cholesterol 10mg; Sodium 70mg; Total Carbohydrate 16g (Dietary Fiber 0g); Protein 1g **Exchanges:** ½ Starch, ½ Other Carbohydrate, 1 Fat **Carbohydrate Choices:** 1

Tip Chopped walnuts are delicious sprinkled on these frosted cookies, or try chopped pecans. Lightly toast them first, if you like, to bring out the flavor.

Ultimate Chocolate-Cappuccino Cookie Cups

Prep Time: 45 Minutes • **Start to Finish:** 1 Hour 15 Minutes • Makes 3 dozen cookies

2 tablespoons cappuccino-flavored instant coffee mix

1 tablespoon water

1 pouch (1 lb 1.5 oz) Betty Crocker double chocolate chunk or chocolate chip cookie mix

3 tablespoons vegetable oil

1 egg

1 container Betty Crocker Rich & Creamy chocolate frosting

1 teaspoon coffee-flavored liqueur

1 cup frozen (thawed) whipped topping

36 chocolate-covered espresso beans

{ Cookie Contest Winner **Linda Bibbo** }

1 Heat oven to 375°F. Line 36 miniature muffin cups with paper baking cups, or spray with cooking spray. In large bowl, dissolve coffee mix in water. Add cookie mix, oil and egg; stir until soft dough forms. Shape dough into 36 (1-inch) balls; place ball in each muffin cup.

2 Bake 8 to 9 minutes or until set. Immediately make indentation in center of each cookie with end of wooden spoon to form a cup. Cool 30 minutes. Remove from pan.

3 In small bowl, stir frosting and liqueur until well blended. Gently stir in whipped topping. Spoon frosting mixture into decorating bag with star tip. Pipe frosting into each cookie cup. Top each with espresso bean. Store covered in refrigerator.

1 Cookie: Calories 170 (Calories from Fat 60); Total Fat 7g (Saturated Fat 2.5g, Trans Fat 1g); Cholesterol 5mg; Sodium 85mg; Total Carbohydrate 27g (Dietary Fiber 0g); Protein 0g **Exchanges:** 2 Other Carbohydrate, 1½ Fat **Carbohydrate Choices:** 2

Tip If you don't have a decorating bag and tip, just put the frosting mixture in a resealable food-storage plastic bag. Snip off a corner, and squeeze the frosting into each baked cookie cup.

Best-Ever Chewy Gingerbread Cookies

Prep Time: 1 Hour 30 Minutes • **Start to Finish:** 3 Hours 30 Minutes • Makes 7½ dozen cookies

- 1 cup plus 2 tablespoons unsalted butter, softened
- 1 cup packed brown sugar
- 1 egg
- ¼ cup plus 2 tablespoons molasses
- 2½ cups Gold Medal all-purpose flour
- 2¼ teaspoons baking soda
- ½ teaspoon kosher (coarse) salt
- 1 tablespoon ground ginger
- 1 tablespoon ground cinnamon
- 2 teaspoons ground cloves
- 1½ teaspoons ground nutmeg
- ½ teaspoon ground allspice
- ⅔ cup granulated or coarse sugar

{ Cookie Contest Winner **Shannon Bills** }

1 In large bowl, beat butter and brown sugar with electric mixer on medium speed until light and fluffy, about 5 minutes. Beat in egg and molasses. Stir in remaining ingredients except granulated sugar. Cover; refrigerate at least 2 hours.

2 Heat oven to 350°F. Line cookie sheets with cooking parchment paper. In small bowl, place granulated sugar. Shape dough into 1-inch balls; roll in sugar. On cookie sheets, place balls about 2 inches apart.

3 Bake 8 to 10 minutes or just until set and soft in center. Cool 2 minutes; remove from cookie sheets to cooling racks. Store tightly covered up to 1 week.

1 Cookie: Calories 50 (Calories from Fat 20); Total Fat 2.5g (Saturated Fat 1.5g, Trans Fat 0g); Cholesterol 10mg; Sodium 45mg; Total Carbohydrate 8g (Dietary Fiber 0g); Protein 0g **Exchanges:** ½ Other Carbohydrate, ½ Fat **Carbohydrate Choices:** ½

Tip Look for cooking parchment paper with the waxed paper, foil and plastic wrap at the grocery store.

Chunky and Nutty

Spumoni Chunk Cookies

Prep Time: 35 Minutes • **Start to Finish:** 50 Minutes • Makes 2 dozen cookies

- 1 pouch (1 lb 1.5 oz) Betty Crocker sugar cookie mix
- ½ cup butter or margarine, softened
- 1 egg
- 1 cup dried cherries, coarsely chopped
- 1 cup semisweet chocolate chunks
- 1 cup salted dry-roasted pistachio nuts, coarsely chopped

{ Cookie Contest Winner **Jayme Fisher** }

1 Heat oven to 375°F. In large bowl, stir cookie mix, butter and egg until soft dough forms. Stir in cherries, chocolate chunks and nuts.

2 Onto ungreased cookie sheets, drop dough by rounded tablespoonfuls about 2 inches apart.

3 Bake 10 to 12 minutes or until edges are golden brown. Cool 2 minutes; remove from cookie sheets to cooling racks. Cool completely.

1 Cookie: Calories 210; Total Fat 10g (Saturated Fat 4.5g, Trans Fat 1g); Cholesterol 20mg; Sodium 110mg; Total Carbohydrate 27g (Dietary Fiber 1g); Protein 2g **Exchanges:** ½ Starch, 1½ Other Carbohydrate, 2 Fat **Carbohydrate Choices:** 2

Tip Can't get enough spumoni? Serve cookies with a dish of spumoni ice cream.

Choco-Cherry Double Delights

Prep Time: 45 Minutes • **Start to Finish:** 1 Hour • Makes 2½ dozen cookies

1⅓ cups whole maraschino cherries, well drained

1 pouch (1 lb 1.5 oz) Betty Crocker double chocolate chunk cookie mix

2 tablespoons vegetable oil

1 tablespoon water

1 egg, beaten

½ cup chopped macadamia nuts

1 teaspoon powdered sugar

{ Cookie Contest Winner **Diana Neves** }

1 Heat oven to 375°F. Cut 15 of the maraschino cherries in half; set aside for topping cookies. Chop remaining cherries.

2 In large bowl, stir cookie mix, oil, water and egg until soft dough forms. Stir in chopped cherries and nuts.

3 Onto ungreased cookie sheets, drop dough by rounded teaspoonfuls about 2 inches apart. Press 1 cherry half lightly into center of each cookie.

4 Bake 7 to 9 minutes or until set. Cool 2 minutes; remove from cookie sheets to cooling racks. Cool completely, about 15 minutes. Before serving, sprinkle with powdered sugar. Store loosely covered at room temperature.

1 Cookie: Calories 110; Total Fat 4g (Saturated Fat 1.5g, Trans Fat 0g); Cholesterol 5mg; Sodium 75mg; Total Carbohydrate 17g (Dietary Fiber 0g); Protein 1g **Exchanges:** ½ Starch, ½ Other Carbohydrate, 1 Fat **Carbohydrate Choices:** 1

Tip Because of their high fat content, macadamia nuts should be stored in the refrigerator or freezer. All types of nuts keep well in the freezer, so you can always be prepared when the cookie-baking bug strikes!

Chunky and Nutty • **13**

Choco-Hazelnut Latte Cookies

Prep Time: 50 Minutes • **Start to Finish:** 1 Hour 10 Minutes • Makes 32 cookies

1 pouch (1 lb 1.5 oz) Betty Crocker sugar cookie mix

⅓ cup unsweetened baking cocoa

3 tablespoons instant coffee granules or crystals

½ cup butter or margarine, softened

3 tablespoons hazelnut-flavored syrup for beverages (from 12.7-oz bottle)

1 egg

1½ cups toasted* hazelnuts, chopped

1 cup miniature semisweet chocolate chips

⅔ cup Betty Crocker Rich & Creamy chocolate frosting (from 1-lb container)

4½ teaspoons hazelnut-flavored syrup for beverages (from 12.7-oz bottle)

{ Cookie Contest Winner **Julie Messmer** }

1 Heat oven to 350°F. In large bowl, stir together cookie mix, cocoa and instant coffee. Add butter, 3 tablespoons syrup and the egg; stir until soft dough forms. Stir in 1 cup of the nuts and the chocolate chips.

2 Onto ungreased cookie sheets, drop dough with rounded 1½-tablespoon-size cookie scoop or by rounded tablespoonfuls 2 inches apart. Press each mound to flatten slightly.

3 Bake 8 to 10 minutes or until set. Cool 3 minutes; remove from cookie sheets to cooling racks. Cool completely, about 15 minutes.

4 In small bowl, stir frosting and 4½ teaspoons syrup. Spread about 1 teaspoon frosting on each cookie. Sprinkle with remaining ½ cup nuts.

*To toast hazelnuts, heat oven to 350°F. Spread nuts in ungreased shallow pan. Bake uncovered 6 to 10 minutes, stirring occasionally, until light brown.

1 Cookie: Calories 190; Total Fat 10g (Saturated Fat 3.5g, Trans Fat 1g); Cholesterol 15mg; Sodium 85mg; Total Carbohydrate 22g (Dietary Fiber 1g); Protein 2g **Exchanges:** ½ Starch, 1 Other Carbohydrate, 2 Fat **Carbohydrate Choices:** 1½

Dark Chocolate–Glazed Orange Macaroons

Prep Time: 1 Hour • **Start to Finish:** 2 Hours 15 Minutes • Makes 2½ dozen macaroons

2⅔ cups firmly packed flaked coconut

⅔ cup sugar

¼ cup Gold Medal all-purpose flour

4 egg whites

½ cup finely chopped pecans

1 tablespoon grated orange peel

2 teaspoons vanilla

½ teaspoon almond extract

3 oz dark baking chocolate, chopped

{ Cookie Contest Winner **Holly Bauer** }

1 Heat oven to 325°F. Line cookie sheets with cooking parchment paper.

2 In large bowl, mix coconut, sugar and flour. Stir in egg whites, pecans, orange peel, vanilla and almond extract. Onto cookie sheet, drop dough by rounded tablespoonfuls about 2 inches apart.

3 Bake 18 to 22 minutes or until golden. Remove from cookie sheets to cooling racks; cool completely.

4 In small resealable freezer plastic bag, place chocolate; seal bag. Microwave on High about 1 minute or until softened. Gently squeeze bag until chocolate is smooth; cut off tiny corner of bag. Squeeze bag to drizzle chocolate over cookies. Let stand until set.

1 Macaroon: Calories 100; Total Fat 5g (Saturated Fat 3.5g, Trans Fat 0g); Cholesterol 0mg; Sodium 30mg; Total Carbohydrate 10g (Dietary Fiber 1g); Protein 1g **Exchanges:** ½ Starch, 1 Fat **Carbohydrate Choices:** ½

Tip When you need to separate an egg, take it out of the refrigerator right before separating, as chilled eggs separate easier.

Butter Pecan Thumbprints

Prep Time: 1 Hour 10 Minutes • **Start to Finish:** 1 Hour 40 Minutes • Makes 3 dozen cookies

{ Cookie Contest Winner **Mary Shivers** }

1 Heat oven to 325°F. Grease cookie sheet with shortening or cooking spray, or line with cooking parchment paper.

2 In large bowl, beat 1 cup brown sugar, ½ cup butter, the egg and vanilla with electric mixer on low speed. Stir in 1½ cups flour, the baking soda and salt. Stir in 1½ cups pecans.

3 In small bowl, mix ⅓ cup brown sugar, 2 tablespoons flour and 1 cup pecans. Stir in 2 tablespoons butter with fork until mixture is crumbly.

4 Shape dough into 1½-inch balls. Place balls about 2 inches apart on cookie sheet. Press thumb into center of each cookie to make indentation, but do not press all the way to the cookie sheet. Fill each indentation with about 1 teaspoon filling.

5 Bake 10 to 15 minutes or until edges are golden brown. Cool 5 minutes; remove from cookie sheets to cooling racks.

Cookies

1 cup packed light brown sugar

½ cup unsalted butter, softened

1 egg, beaten

2 teaspoons vanilla

1½ cups Gold Medal all-purpose flour

¼ teaspoon baking soda

⅛ teaspoon kosher (coarse) salt

1½ cups finely chopped pecans

Filling

⅓ cup packed light brown sugar

2 tablespoons Gold Medal all-purpose flour

1 cup finely chopped pecans

2 tablespoons unsalted butter, softened

1 Cookie: Calories 150; Total Fat 9g (Saturated Fat 2.5g, Trans Fat 0g); Cholesterol 15mg; Sodium 20mg; Total Carbohydrate 16g (Dietary Fiber 1g); Protein 1g **Exchanges:** 1 Other Carbohydrate, 2 Fat **Carbohydrate Choices:** 1

Tip Use a thimble or the end of a wooden spoon to make uniform indentations in cookie dough.

Pumpkin-Pecan Spice Cookies

Prep Time: 1 Hour 5 Minutes • **Start to Finish:** 1 Hour 35 Minutes • Makes 3½ dozen cookies

1½ cups packed light brown sugar

½ cup butter or margarine, softened

2 eggs

½ cup canned pumpkin (not pumpkin pie mix)

3 teaspoons vanilla

2¾ cups Gold Medal all-purpose flour

2 teaspoons baking powder

1 teaspoon ground cinnamon

½ teaspoon salt

½ teaspoon ground ginger

¼ teaspoon ground nutmeg

⅛ teaspoon ground allspice

⅛ teaspoon ground cloves

Pinch ground cardamom

1⅓ cups finely chopped pecans

½ cup white vanilla baking chips

4 oz vanilla-flavored candy coating (almond bark), chopped

{ Cookie Contest Winner **Debra Keil** }

1 Heat oven to 350°F. Grease cookie sheet with shortening or cooking spray, or line with cooking parchment paper.

2 In large bowl, beat brown sugar, butter, eggs, pumpkin and vanilla with electric mixer on medium speed. Stir in flour, baking powder and spices. Stir in pecans and baking chips. Onto cookie sheet, drop dough by rounded tablespoonfuls about 2 inches apart.

3 Bake 10 to 14 minutes or until edges are lightly browned. Remove from cookie sheets to cooling racks. Cool completely, about 30 minutes.

4 Place candy coating in small resealable freezer plastic bag; seal bag. Microwave on High about 1 minute or until softened. Gently squeeze bag until coating is smooth; cut off tiny corner of bag. Squeeze bag to drizzle coating over cookies. Let stand until set.

1 Cookie: Calories 140; Total Fat 7g (Saturated Fat 3g, Trans Fat 0g); Cholesterol 15mg; Sodium 80mg; Total Carbohydrate 18g (Dietary Fiber 0g); Protein 2g **Exchanges:** 1 Other Carbohydrate, 1½ Fat **Carbohydrate Choices: 1**

Tip When buying canned pumpkin, check the label to be sure it's not pumpkin pie mix, which contains sugar and spices.

Chunky and Nutty

Crispy and Crunchy

Caramel Macchiato Thumbprints

Prep Time: 55 Minutes • **Start to Finish:** 1 Hour 25 Minutes • Makes 3 dozen cookies

{ Cookie Contest Winner **Edwina Gadsby** }

1 Heat oven to 375°F. In large bowl, dissolve coffee powder in hot water. Stir in cookie mix, flour, butter, vanilla and egg until very soft dough forms.

2 Shape dough into 1½-inch balls. On ungreased cookie sheets, place balls about 2 inches apart. Using thumb or handle of wooden spoon, make indentation in center of each cookie.

- 2 teaspoons instant espresso coffee powder or granules
- 1 tablespoon hot water
- 1 pouch (1 lb 1.5 oz) Betty Crocker sugar cookie mix
- ¼ cup Gold Medal all-purpose flour
- ½ cup butter or margarine, melted
- 2 teaspoons vanilla
- 1 egg
- 18 caramels (from 14-oz bag), unwrapped
- 2 tablespoons milk
- ½ cup semisweet chocolate chips
- 1 teaspoon shortening

3 Bake 8 to 10 minutes or until edges are light golden brown. Cool 2 minutes; remove from cookie sheets to cooling racks.

4 In small microwavable bowl, microwave caramels and milk uncovered on High 1 minute to 1 minute 30 seconds, stirring once, until caramels are melted. Spoon ½ teaspoon caramel into indentation in each cookie. Cool 15 minutes.

5 In another small microwavable bowl, microwave chocolate chips and shortening uncovered on High 1 minute to 1 minute 30 seconds or until chips can be stirred smooth. Drizzle chocolate over cookies. Let stand about 30 minutes or until chocolate is set.

1 Cookie: Calories 120; Total Fat 5g (Saturated Fat 2.5g, Trans Fat 0.5g); Cholesterol 15mg; Sodium 75mg; Total Carbohydrate 17g (Dietary Fiber 0g); Protein 1g **Exchanges:** ½ Starch, ½ Other Carbohydrate, 1 Fat **Carbohydrate Choices:** 1

Tip To drizzle chocolate easily, spoon melted chocolate into small resealable food-storage plastic bag; cut small tip from 1 bottom corner. Squeeze bag gently to drizzle chocolate over cookies.

Black-and-White Coconut Macaroons

Prep Time: 1 Hour • **Start to Finish:** 2 Hours 25 Minutes • Makes 40 macaroons

{ Cookie Contest Winner **Judie Hampton** }

1 Heat oven to 350°F. Line cookie sheets with cooking parchment paper. Using food processor, process coconut until finely ground.

2 In large bowl, stir together coconut and cookie mix. Add sweetened condensed milk and almond extract; mix well. Mixture will be crumbly. Stir in cream of tartar.

3 In small bowl, beat egg whites with electric mixer on medium speed until soft peaks form. Fold egg whites into cookie mixture. Using 1½-tablespoon-size cookie scoop, firmly pack with coconut mixture and place mound on cookie sheet. Repeat with remaining coconut, placing mounds about 2 inches apart. Press each mound to flatten slightly.

4 Bake 8 to 10 minutes or until edges just begin to lightly brown (do not overbake). Cool 2 minutes; remove from cookie sheets to cooling racks. Cool completely, about 15 minutes.

5 In 1-quart nonstick saucepan, melt chocolate chips and shortening over medium heat, stirring until chocolate is melted. Dip each cooled cookie halfway into melted chocolate, letting excess drip off. Place on sheet of parchment paper; sprinkle chocolate portion with nuts. Let stand until chocolate sets, about 1 hour. Store between sheets of parchment paper in tightly covered container.

Cookies
- 3 cups lightly packed shredded coconut
- 1 pouch (1 lb 1.5 oz) Betty Crocker sugar cookie mix
- ½ cup sweetened condensed milk (not evaporated)
- ½ to 1 teaspoon almond extract
- 1 teaspoon cream of tartar
- 2 egg whites

Glaze
- 2 cups semisweet chocolate chips (12 oz)
- 1 tablespoon shortening
- ⅓ cup macadamia nuts, finely chopped

1 Macaroon: Calories 160; Total Fat 8g (Saturated Fat 4.5g, Trans Fat 0.5g); Cholesterol 0mg; Sodium 65mg; Total Carbohydrate 20g (Dietary Fiber 1g); Protein 1g **Exchanges:** 1½ Other Carbohydrate, 1½ Fat **Carbohydrate Choices:** 1

Tip It's easy to line cookie sheets with cooking parchment paper for even baking, no sticking and no cleanup.

Linzer Cookie Tarts

Prep Time: 1 Hour 15 Minutes • **Start to Finish:** 2 Hours • Makes 32 cookies

1 pouch (1 lb 1.5 oz) Betty Crocker sugar cookie mix
⅓ cup slivered almonds, toasted*, finely chopped
⅓ cup butter or margarine, melted
½ teaspoon almond extract
1 egg
⅔ cup seedless raspberry jam
⅓ cup dark or semisweet chocolate chips

{ Cookie Contest Winner **Jane Hazen** }

1 Heat oven to 375°F. In large bowl, stir cookie mix and almonds until mixed. Stir in melted butter, almond extract and egg until stiff dough forms.

2 On floured surface, roll half of dough to ¼-inch thickness. Cut with 2-inch round, fluted or star cookie cutter. On ungreased cookie sheets, place cookies about 2 inches apart.

3 Bake 7 to 9 minutes or until set. Cool 5 minutes; remove from cookie sheets to cooling racks. Cool completely.

4 Meanwhile, on floured surface, roll other half of dough to ¼-inch thickness. Cut with linzer cutter with hole in center, OR cut with same 2-inch round cookie cutter and use small 1-inch cutter to cut round hole out of center of each cookie. On ungreased cookie sheets, place cookies about 2 inches apart.

5 Bake 7 to 9 minutes or until set. Cool 5 minutes; remove from cookie sheets to cooling racks. Cool completely.

6 Spread 1 teaspoon jam on bottom of each whole cookie; top each with cutout cookie to make sandwich cookie. In small microwavable bowl, microwave chocolate chips uncovered on High about 1 minute, stirring after 30 seconds, until melted and stirred smooth. Using tip of fork or knife, drizzle chocolate in lines over cookies. Let stand until chocolate is set, about 45 minutes. Or, sprinkle with powdered sugar instead of drizzling with chocolate. Store between sheets of waxed paper in tightly covered container.

*To toast almonds, sprinkle in ungreased shallow pan. Bake uncovered at 350°F 6 to 10 minutes, stirring occasionally, until golden brown.

1 Cookie: Calories 120; Total Fat 4.5g (Saturated Fat 2g, Trans Fat 0.5g); Cholesterol 10mg; Sodium 55mg; Total Carbohydrate 18g (Dietary Fiber 0g); Protein 1g **Exchanges:** ½ Starch, ½ Other Carbohydrate, 1 Fat **Carbohydrate Choices:** 1

Summer Celebration Lemonade Biscotti

Prep Time: 30 Minutes • **Start to Finish:** 1 Hours 35 Minutes • Makes 16 biscotti

½ cup butter or margarine, melted

¼ cup frozen lemonade concentrate, thawed

2 teaspoons grated lemon peel

1 teaspoon lemon extract

2 eggs

1 pouch (1 lb 1.5 oz) Betty Crocker sugar cookie mix

1½ cups Gold Medal all-purpose flour

½ cup chopped dried cherries

{ Cookie Contest Winner **Mary Hawkes** }

1 Heat oven to 350°F. Line large cookie sheet with foil. In large bowl, stir butter, lemonade concentrate, lemon peel, lemon extract and eggs until well mixed. Add remaining ingredients; stir until soft dough forms.

2 Divide dough in half. On cookie sheet, shape each half of dough into a 12 x 2-inch log.

3 Bake 25 to 30 minutes or until edges are golden brown. Cool 15 minutes.

4 Carefully lift foil to move cookie logs to cutting board. With serrated knife, carefully cut each log crosswise on a slight diagonal into ¾-inch slices. Place slices cut side down on cookie sheet.

5 Bake 15 to 20 minutes, gently turning cookies over once during baking. Cool 2 minutes; remove from cookie sheet to cooling rack. Cool completely. Store loosely covered at room temperature.

1 Biscotti: Calories 130; Total Fat 4.5g (Saturated Fat 2g, Trans Fat 0.5g); Cholesterol 20mg; Sodium 70mg; Total Carbohydrate 19g (Dietary Fiber 0g); Protein 1g **Exchanges:** 1½ Other Carbohydrate, 1 Fat **Carbohydrate Choices:** 1

Tip Sprinkle baked biscotti with powdered sugar for a special touch.

Memory Lane Oatmeal–Peanut Butter Creme Sandwiches

Prep Time: 1 Hour • **Start to Finish:** 1 Hour 15 Minutes • Makes 20 sandwich cookies

Cookies
1 pouch (1 lb 1.5 oz) Betty Crocker oatmeal cookie mix
¼ cup packed brown sugar
½ cup butter or margarine, softened
½ cup creamy peanut butter
1 tablespoon water
1 egg

Filling
1 cup creamy peanut butter
½ cup Betty Crocker Rich & Creamy vanilla frosting
4 teaspoons milk

{ Cookie Contest Winner **Nancy Elliot** }

1 Heat oven to 375°F. In large bowl, stir cookie mix, brown sugar, butter, ½ cup peanut butter, the water and egg until soft dough forms.

2 Roll dough into 40 (1¼-inch) balls. On ungreased cookie sheets, place balls about 2 inches apart. Press with fingers to slightly flatten.

3 Bake 9 to 10 minutes or until light golden brown. Cool 3 minutes; remove from cookie sheets to cooling racks. Cool completely, about 15 minutes.

4 In small bowl, stir all filling ingredients until well blended. For each sandwich cookie, spread about 1 tablespoon filling on bottom of 1 cookie; top with another cookie, bottom side down. Press together lightly, twisting slightly. Store tightly covered at room temperature.

1 Sandwich Cookie: Calories 300; Total Fat 17g (Saturated Fat 5g, Trans Fat 0.5g); Cholesterol 25mg; Sodium 230mg; Total Carbohydrate 31g (Dietary Fiber 1g); Protein 7g **Exchanges:** 1 Starch, 1 Other Carbohydrate, ½ Medium-Fat Meat, 3 Fat **Carbohydrate Choices:** 2

Tip Spray your measuring cup with cooking spray before measuring the peanut butter, and the peanut butter will slide right out!

Alfajores (Dulce de Leche Sandwich Creme Cookies)

Prep Time: 1 Hour 20 Minutes • **Start to Finish:** 1 Hour 20 Minutes • Makes 2 dozen sandwich cookies

- 1 pouch (1 lb 1.5 oz) Betty Crocker sugar cookie mix
- 1 cup coconut
- ½ cup pecan halves, toasted*, finely chopped
- ⅓ cup butter or margarine, melted
- 1 egg
- 1 can (13.4 oz) dulce de leche (caramelized sweetened condensed milk)
- 2 tablespoons powdered sugar

{ Cookie Contest Winner **Christine Montalvo** }

1 Heat oven to 375°F. Line cookie sheets with cooking parchment paper.

2 In large bowl, stir cookie mix, ½ cup of the coconut, the pecans, melted butter and egg until stiff dough forms.

3 On floured surface, roll half of dough to ¼-inch thickness. Cut with 2-inch round or fluted cookie cutter. On cookie sheets, place cookies about 2 inches apart. Repeat with remaining half of dough.

4 Bake 7 to 9 minutes or until set. Cool 2 minutes; remove from cookie sheets to cooling racks. Cool completely.

5 To make each sandwich cookie, spread about 2 teaspoons dulce de leche on bottom of 1 cookie. Top with second cookie, bottom side down; gently press cookies together so some of filling seeps out around edges. Roll edges in remaining ½ cup coconut. Place cookies on cooling racks.

6 Sprinkle tops of sandwich cookies with powdered sugar. Store between sheets of waxed paper in tightly covered container.

1 Sandwich Cookie: Calories 190; Total Fat 8g (Saturated Fat 4g, Trans Fat 1g); Cholesterol 15mg; Sodium 95mg; Total Carbohydrate 28g (Dietary Fiber 0g); Protein 3g **Exchanges:** ½ Starch, 1½ Other Carbohydrate, 1½ Fat **Carbohydrate Choices:** 2

* To toast pecans, sprinkle in ungreased shallow pan. Bake uncovered at 350°F 6 to 10 minutes, stirring occasionally, until golden brown.

Iced Cinnamon-Pecan Biscotti

Prep Time: 40 Minutes • **Start to Finish:** 2 Hours 15 Minutes • Makes 16 biscotti

{ Cookie Contest Winner **Christine Yang** }

1 Heat oven to 350°F. Line cookie sheet with cooking parchment paper. In medium bowl, mix flour, baking powder and 1 teaspoon cinnamon.

2 In large bowl, beat granulated sugar, salt and ½ cup softened butter with electric mixer on medium speed until light and fluffy. Add 1 teaspoon vanilla. Beat in eggs, one at a time, until well blended. Gradually add flour mixture, beating until well blended.

3 Place dough on cookie sheet. With floured fingers, press dough into 14 x 10-inch rectangle. In small bowl, mix brown sugar, ¼ cup softened butter, 1 teaspoon cinnamon and ¾ cup of the pecans. Spread brown sugar mixture evenly over dough to within ½ inch of edges of dough. Using parchment paper to lift dough, fold long sides of dough over center third of dough, overlapping one side over the other. Shape dough into 12 x 3-inch log. Press remaining ¼ cup pecans on top.

4 Bake 28 to 30 minutes or until light golden brown. Cool on cookie sheet 15 minutes. Leaving baked cookie on parchment paper, carefully remove from cookie sheet onto cutting board. Using serrated knife, cut crosswise into ¾-inch slices. Carefully place slices cut side down on cookie sheet. Bake 15 to 18 minutes or until light golden brown. Cool completely on cookie sheet, about 30 minutes.

5 In small bowl, stir powdered sugar and milk until mixed. Add corn syrup and ¼ teaspoon vanilla; blend until smooth. Drizzle over cooled biscotti.

Cookies
- 2 cups Gold Medal all-purpose flour
- 1½ teaspoons baking powder
- 1 teaspoon ground cinnamon
- ½ cup granulated sugar
- ¼ teaspoon salt
- ½ cup unsalted butter or regular butter, softened
- 1 teaspoon vanilla
- 2 eggs

Filling
- ½ cup packed brown sugar
- ¼ cup unsalted butter or regular butter, softened
- 1 teaspoon ground cinnamon
- 1 cup toasted* pecans, chopped

Icing
- ½ cup powdered sugar
- 2 teaspoons milk
- 1 teaspoon light corn syrup
- ¼ teaspoon vanilla

1 Biscotti: Calories 270; Total Fat 15g (Saturated Fat 6g, Trans Fat 0g); Cholesterol 50mg; Sodium 120mg; Total Carbohydrate 30g (Dietary Fiber 1g); Protein 3g **Exchanges:** 1 Starch, 1 Other Carbohydrate, 3 Fat **Carbohydrate Choices:** 2

* To toast pecans, sprinkle in ungreased shallow pan. Bake uncovered at 350°F 6 to 10 minutes, stirring occasionally, until golden brown.

Mega-Bucks Shortbread

Prep Time: 20 Minutes • **Start to Finish:** 2 Hours 20 Minutes • Makes 36 bars

¾ cup butter, softened

¼ cup packed brown sugar

1½ cups Gold Medal all-purpose flour

½ teaspoon salt

½ cup chopped dry-roasted macadamia nuts

1 can (14 oz) sweetened condensed milk (not evaporated)

1 bag (12 oz) white vanilla baking chips (2 cups)

4 oz dried pineapple, finely chopped (¾ cup)

1 bag (12 oz) semisweet chocolate chips (2 cups)

1 tablespoon butter

¼ cup whipping cream

{ Cookie Contest Winner **Lori Falce** }

1 Heat oven to 350°F. In medium bowl, beat ¾ cup softened butter and the brown sugar until creamy. Add flour and salt; mix until soft dough forms. Stir in nuts. Press in ungreased 9-inch square pan. Bake 25 to 30 minutes or until light golden brown. Cool 10 minutes.

2 In medium microwavable bowl, microwave sweetened condensed milk and vanilla baking chips uncovered on High 1 to 2 minutes, stirring every 30 seconds, until chips are completely melted and mixture is smooth. Stir in dried pineapple. Pour over shortbread in pan. Refrigerate about 1 hour 30 minutes or until set.

3 In small microwavable bowl, microwave chocolate chips, 1 tablespoon butter and the whipping cream uncovered on High 1 to 2 minutes, stirring every 30 seconds, until chips are completely melted. Spread over pineapple layer. Refrigerate about 1 hour or until set. For bars, cut into 6 rows by 6 rows. Store covered in refrigerator.

1 Bar: Calories 220; Total Fat 12g (Saturated Fat 8g, Trans Fat 0g); Cholesterol 15mg; Sodium 100mg; Total Carbohydrate 26g (Dietary Fiber 1g); Protein 2g **Exchanges:** ½ Starch, 1 Other Carbohydrate, 2½ Fat **Carbohydrate Choices:** 2

Tip To cut bars easily, line bottom and sides of 9-inch square pan with foil, leaving foil overhanging at 2 opposite sides of pan. Make bars as directed. Use foil to lift bars from pan, then pull foil from sides of bars before cutting.

Metric Conversion Guide

Volume

U.S. Units	Canadian Metric	Australian Metric
¼ teaspoon	1 mL	1 ml
½ teaspoon	2 mL	2 ml
1 teaspoon	5 mL	5 ml
1 tablespoon	15 mL	20 ml
¼ cup	50 mL	60 ml
⅓ cup	75 mL	80 ml
½ cup	125 mL	125 ml
⅔ cup	150 mL	170 ml
¾ cup	175 mL	190 ml
1 cup	250 mL	250 ml
1 quart	1 liter	1 liter
1½ quarts	1.5 liters	1.5 liters
2 quarts	2 liters	2 liters
2½ quarts	2.5 liters	2.5 liters
3 quarts	3 liters	3 liters
4 quarts	4 liters	4 liters

Weight

U.S. Units	Canadian Metric	Australian Metric
1 ounce	30 grams	30 grams
2 ounces	55 grams	60 grams
3 ounces	85 grams	90 grams
4 ounces (¼ pound)	115 grams	125 grams
8 ounces (½ pound)	225 grams	225 grams
16 ounces (1 pound)	455 grams	500 grams
1 pound	455 grams	0.5 kilogram

Note: The recipes in this cookbook have not been developed or tested using metric measures. When converting recipes to metric, some variations in quality may be noted.

Measurements

Inches	Centimeters
1	2.5
2	5.0
3	7.5
4	10.0
5	12.5
6	15.0
7	17.5
8	20.5
9	23.0
10	25.5
11	28.0
12	30.5
13	33.0

Temperatures

Fahrenheit	Celsius
32°	0°
212°	100°
250°	120°
275°	140°
300°	150°
325°	160°
350°	180°
375°	190°
400°	200°
425°	220°
450°	230°
475°	240°
500°	260°

Recipe Testing and Calculating Nutrition Information

Recipe Testing:

- Large eggs and 2% milk were used unless otherwise indicated.
- Fat-free, low-fat, low-sodium or lite products were not used unless indicated.
- No nonstick cookware and bakeware were used unless otherwise indicated. No dark-colored, black or insulated bakeware was used.
- When a pan is specified, a metal pan was used; a baking dish or pie plate means ovenproof glass was used.
- An electric hand mixer was used for mixing only when mixer speeds are specified.

Calculating Nutrition:

- The first ingredient was used wherever a choice is given, such as ⅓ cup sour cream or plain yogurt.
- The first amount was used wherever a range is given, such as 3- to 3½-pound whole chicken.
- The first serving number was used wherever a range is given, such as 4 to 6 servings.
- "If desired" ingredients were not included.
- Only the amount of a marinade or frying oil that is absorbed was included.

America's most trusted cookbook is better than ever!

- 1,100 all-new photos, including hundreds of step-by-step images
- More than 1,500 recipes, with hundreds of inspiring variations and creative "mini" recipes for easy cooking ideas
- Brand-new features
- Gorgeous new design

Get the best edition of the *Betty Crocker Cookbook* today!

www.ingramcontent.com/pod-product-compliance
Lightning Source LLC
Chambersburg PA
CBHW071418290426
44108CB00014B/1879